# Please Grow Up!

*Reuben Egolf*

Copyright © 2014 Reuben Egolf
All rights reserved.

ISBN: 1505383137
ISBN 13: 9781505383133
Library of Congress Control Number: 2014921825
CreateSpace Independent Pub. Platform,
North Charleston, South Carolina

# Table of Contents

**Chapter One** . . . . . . . . . . . . . . . . . . . . . . . . . . . . .1
What Is Maturity?

**Chapter Two** . . . . . . . . . . . . . . . . . . . . . . . . . . . . .11
How to Build Integrity

**Chapter Three** . . . . . . . . . . . . . . . . . . . . . . . . . .19
The Behaviors of Maturity

**Chapter Four** . . . . . . . . . . . . . . . . . . . . . . . . . . .51
The Agents God Uses for Growth

**About the Author** . . . . . . . . . . . . . . . . . . . . . . . .59

## CHAPTER ONE

# What Is Maturity?

*Maturity: Be able to stick with a job until it is finished. Be able to bear an injustice without having to get even. Be able to carry money without spending it. Do your duty without being supervised.*
—Ann Landers

Maturity is the state of being fully developed or fully grown. It is the process of going from a self-centered world to esteeming others as equal in value. Nothing illustrates this process any better than watching a child grow from his or her days in the crib to the teenage years. A child's world revolves around his- or herself day and night, but through parental correction and exposure to others, the child's attitude changes to, "This is not all about me."

## Please Grow Up!

"Consider this story told by Bernard L. Brown Jr., president of the Kennestone Regional Health Care System in the state of Georgia. Brown once worked in a hospital where a patient knocked over a cup of water, which spilled on the floor beside the patient's bed. The patient was afraid he might slip on the water if he got out of the bed, so he asked a nurse's aide to mop it up. The patient didn't know it, but the hospital policy said that small spills were the responsibility of the nurse's aides while large spills were to be mopped up by the hospital's housekeeping group. The nurse's aide decided the spill was a large one and she called the housekeeping department. A housekeeper arrived and declared the spill a small one. An argument followed.

"'It's not my responsibility,' said the nurse's aide, 'because it's a large puddle.' The housekeeper did not agree. 'Well, it's not mine,' she said. 'The puddle is too small.'

"The exasperated patient listened for a time, then took a pitcher of water from his night table and poured the whole thing on the floor. 'Is that a big enough puddle now for you two to decide?'

he asked. It was, and that was the end of the argument."[1]

We have all heard the age-old advice of parents telling a child, in no uncertain terms, "Grow up!" Usually the parent will say it in an urgent tone to convey that the sooner it happens, the better. Immaturity is costly and reduces the effectiveness of a person and a church. We create all kinds of problems by saying immature things, by making immature decisions, and by acting in immature ways. The result is hurt feelings, loss of friendships, division in families and churches, and, ultimately, the loss of effectiveness in winning the world to Christ. We have all seen a driver passing impatiently and making obscene hand signals as he passed us—and then noticed the "I love Jesus" bumper sticker. The immature behavior of that person ruins the witness of the bumper sticker. We all have walked away from situations saying to ourselves, "Why did I say that?" However, as we mature, those moments of regret should happen less and less often.

---

[1] *Bits & Pieces*, September 16, 1993, 22–24.

## Please Grow Up!

Growing older is inevitable, but growing up is an option! Spiritual maturity takes time, effort, dedication, and humility. We cannot microwave ourselves to maturity. It is a slow-cooking process of development; no one arrives at maturity overnight. We arrive at maturity not accidentally, but on purpose. Maturity is a lifestyle of diligence in creating the future with each decision we make. No one arrives at the top of a mountain accidentally and wonders, "How did this happen?" Reaching the top takes effort, planning, and intent. Circumventing this process is like building on sand. With time, we can dig below the sand and hit rock. But if impatience is the route we take, then we will deceive ourselves and hurriedly build on top of that which should have been removed. Maturity should be a goal of life. We don't think of it as a goal; we think of owning a house, having a career, having children, and retiring as goals. However, without maturity, none of these other goals will truly be appreciated or perhaps even achieved.

What is maturity? It means to be fully developed, full grown, and able to fulfill our created purpose. Maturity is being able to balance the short-term gains against the long-term consequences.

Growing up is the process of leaving childhood behind, embracing adulthood and all it represents, such as responsibility and an awareness that we are not the center of the universe. The greatest revelation of my life was when I came to the cross and realized it wasn't all about me. Maturing is gaining more of Jesus and less of stunting his desires and will in our lives by our fleshly interferences.

When we arrive at maturity, we weigh the pros and cons of our actions and proceed accordingly. Joshua Liebman says, "Maturity is achieved when a person postpones immediate pleasures for long-term values."

## Patient Growth

> But grow in grace, and in the knowledge of our Lord and Savior Jesus Christ...
> **—2 Pet. 3:18**

One of the things Satan loves to do to the church is to rob it of its power to mature. The reason is that the more mature a church becomes, the stronger it becomes. The more it resists against the devil, the more it becomes a testimony to the world. The more it is able to be used by Jesus Christ, the more it becomes a looming giant in the forces of good against satanic power and darkness.

I read a parable about the Chinese bamboo tree and found it to be a beautiful study in maturity. For four years after planting the seed of this tree, the grower gets no satisfaction other than a tiny shoot coming out of a bulb. If he or she didn't know about the growth patterns for this tree, the grower would think that all efforts to plant and cultivate had been useless. But, in fact, what's happening all the time is that underneath the ground a massive root structure is forming. Then, in the fifth year, the Chinese bamboo tree grows and grows and grows, sometimes up to eighty feet tall! People say, "Wow! Isn't that amazing how that thing grows? It's growing overnight." The reality is, it didn't grow overnight. It spent a lot of years in preparation so it could handle the aboveground experience and the eighty feet on top of it. How many people grow eighty feet with no foundation, and they fall out of relationships with Jesus after one year? Maturity is a necessity if spiritual longevity is to be enjoyed.

We live in a microwavable time. We detest waiting and bemoan it as a waste of time in this modern, technological world. We are satisfied with lower quality if we can get what we want faster—hence, the huge success of McDonald's. The sad part is that this mind-set has crept into the church over the last fifty years. People spend less time than ever at the altar because it takes time to develop relationship and quality. Now they have become satisfied with a low quality of spiritual life since it means they can microwave their experience in church to one hour and no more. They have settled for a spiritual Big Mac, but if they had spent a little more time, they could have experienced the spiritual Triple Prime Burger from Ruby Tuesday. There are no shortcuts to revival. If we are going to get spiritual quality back in the church again, it will take time: time spent in prayer, time spent in the word, time spent in fasting, and time spent in corporate worship. Quality is worth waiting for!

Maturity is being able to understand and adapt to the fact that change is a predictable reality on earth. Things are changing all around the world. There's natural seasonal change that happens: summertime, autumn, winter, and around to spring, and back to summer. There are natural changes in weather and temperature. We deal with these changes constantly.

## Please Grow Up!

Do you know that mankind is the only creature of all creation that has the power to determine or design the change he or she desires? I'm not talking physically. I'm not talking about taking back gray hair or putting more hair on the head. We need to realize that it's a dangerous power we have been given, and we should take it seriously. Animals function on instinct, but humans do not. Why? Because we as humans have the power of free will, which means we have the power to make a decision. Animals don't function that way. The groundhogs in the backyard do not have a committee meeting at night to make decisions about how they're going to tear your yard up. They operate on instinct: "I'm hungry. I have to go eat." *Bam!* Out they go.

We sometimes see possums getting run over on the road as a result of not making good decisions. Why? Because they function on instinct: "I have to get to the other side of the road." Here comes a big semi, but they don't even think about it. They're going to the other side to get whatever they're after, but we are not supposed to be like that.

We as people function on intentions. That means we can determine the world we live in. Right now, we Americans are making our own decisions on the world we want to live in. We have the power to determine what is right and wrong. Man has the power to determine what is good and what is bad. We make the decision whether we will love God or curse God. We will either embrace truth or create our own truth. The change is in our hands. America is making decisions not to embrace God but to curse God, but the Bible says, "If you curse God," like Job's wife, "you die."

The book of Psalms says, "If a nation forgets God, they'll be turned into hell." We cannot think we are going to run away from God and create our own truth. Romans 1 states that they literally came up with their own truth and became wise in their own eyes, and God thought they were as dumb as stumps. He is the all knower—not us! The power to mature, first of all, starts with our decision making. Maturity doesn't just happen. Physically growing older is not an option, but growing up is!

The most practical and powerful way to get believers headed in the direction of spiritual maturity is to help them establish habits that promote spiritual growth. We cannot talk about character without talking about habits. Character is the way we habitually act. For example, if we are honest only part of the time, or if we are honest only when we consciously choose to be honest, we cannot claim to have integrity.

Having integrity means we are always honest. It is our habit. We don't even have to think about it. When someone asks us a question or gives us back too much change, we habitually do the honest thing.

> So we continue to preach Christ to each person, using all wisdom to warn and to teach everyone, in order to bring each one into God's presence as a mature person in Christ.
> **—Col. 1:28 (NCV)**

**CHAPTER TWO**

# How to Build Integrity

*If thou faint in the day of adversity, thy strength is small.*
—*Prov. 24:10*

What do we mean when we talk about the integrity of a building? After a large earthquake, we cannot go in that building because its integrity has been compromised. Integrity is the amount of pressure something can take without caving in, falling down, and being compromised.

Life is full of problems, and a big part of life is problem solving. The question to ask is, "Do I have the right attitude as I approach the problems of life?" The Bible tells us, "Count it all joy when you fall into various trials." All of us have problems in this life; all of us have trials; all of us face situations that are not good. How do we handle them? How do we cope with being dealt a bad hand? Do problems throw us for a loop? Do we grumble and gripe? Do we get negative or nervous?

The first test of spiritual maturity is how do we act under pressure? Remember, the Bible says: "Count it all joy when you fall into various trials." Wilting under pressure is an indicator of low integrity and strength. Trials and tests are designed to reveal what's hidden inside a person. Our reactions are symptoms of a cause. Often we make the mistake of dealing only with the symptoms and not with the cause. Physically, we do the same thing, taking medication to dull the pain, but if we dealt with the cause, the recurring symptoms would cease. Pride explains away symptoms and hides its insecurities, while humility permits God's correction to discipline the heart—the cause.

The following five steps help build integrity.

## 1. Live in consistent obedience to known biblical truth.

Integrity is not born; it is made by consistent living in obedience. Each act of obedience builds and strengthens the integrity of our lives. Every time we obey, we build spiritual momentum for the next moment that requires a decision to obey or not. After a while, obedience becomes such a practice and way of life that we obey without thinking about it. Consistently obeying God's word will strengthen the integrity of our spirit and fortify us against compromise.

## 2. Make private life consistent with public life.

The word *hypocrite* comes from the Greek word for *actor*—someone who pretends to be something or someone he is not. Hypocrisy makes it impossible to have integrity. It creates an image in public that requires constant effort, and it eventually tires the spirit and weakens the integrity—the structure and fortification—of the soul. Hypocrisy eventually collapses the person into a state of misery. Living a lie is the hardest thing on earth to do!

The opposite of being a hypocrite is being sincere. In Greek, the word for *sincere* is a compound word that means "without wax." It means "pure," so a sincere act is one motivated out of purity (1 Cor. 13), without regard to self-benefit. If a man sees someone in danger and rescues the person without ever thinking of himself, that is sincerity. If my private life is so different from my public life that they appear to be two different lives, then I am not sincere in my relationship with God. It indicates that my life is filled with the wax of self, and this insincerity is hindering the work of Christ from being seen. When we live what we profess, our public influence on others substantially increases. When we speak what we are living, we speak with a conviction that would not be present if we were living a hypocritical life. When Jesus had finished speaking one day, the people said that unlike the Pharisees, he spoke with authority. This man was sincere, so when he spoke, his words came from a place of deep conviction.

How peaceful it is to live a sincere life! When we have to keep up with the latest lie we've told, life wears us out. Insincerity robs us of sleep, torments our mind, increases fear, and eventually produces a breakdown in body as well as mind.

A hypocrite lacks conviction about what he truly believes and is totally dependent on the opinions of people. That's a person nobody can trust. An individual who lives in private what he projects in public is living by a standard of convictions. Such a person has a value system. Prioritizing is placing things in order of importance and making decisions based upon what is important. What determines this list of importance? Our value system becomes the structure that determines our decisions. A life, like a house, is built on something, and our life is built on a value system.

## 3. Make a practice of being faithful in little things.

> He that is faithful in that which is least is faithful also in much: and he that is unjust in the least is unjust also in much.
>
> If therefore ye have not been faithful in the unrighteous mammon, who will commit to your trust the true riches?
>
> And if ye have not been faithful in that which is another man's, who shall give you that which is your own?
> **—Luke 16:10–12 (KJV)**

Integrity doesn't magically appear the moment someone makes it big, but rather it is painstakingly built in the halls of obscurity in one's life. If we value our reputation enough to act honestly with another person's dollar, then when we are entrusted with their hundred dollars, our integrity will maintain the same responsibility. We have all heard that "practice makes perfect." The more we practice, the more we develop. The more we develop our strength in the small things, the stronger we become in resisting the temptations that increase in the big things. In other words, our strength of character must increase to withstand the growing intensity of temptation that assails increased responsibility.

### 4. Look in the mirror daily and take personal responsibility for failures.

We often create our own misery and then blame everyone else. It's as if we create our own storm and then complain because it rains. When we mature, we accept responsibility. Excuses are shields put up to deflect personal responsibility. As long as we blame everyone else for our failures, there will be no opportunity for us to change. Maturity requires change, and correction is the means to facilitate it. The moment we take responsibility for our behavior is the moment our life begins to change.

## 5. Be humble and learn from mistakes.

Acknowledging that we have made a mistake is the first step, but then we need to learn from the mistake. Humility realizes its own imperfection and inability. In other words, humility is taking a sane view of ourselves, while pride is taking an insane view of ourselves. Pride exaggerates our ability and focuses on self-dependence, but humility realizes its own inefficiency and focuses on God for continued dependence. Whatever we focus on for strength becomes our source. When self is the focus, then our strength is finite and very limited in dealing with the issues of life. However, when we focus on Christ as our source, then our strength becomes infinite and unlimited. God can correct us through many methods, such as an inner witness, another person, his word, or circumstances. Being humble means we yield to the correction and permit his hand to form and stretch us into being more like Jesus.

**CHAPTER THREE**

# The Behaviors of Maturity

*Don't mix bad words with your bad mood. You'll have many opportunities to change a mood, but you'll never get the opportunity to replace the words you spoke.*

—*Nishan Panwar*

Many years ago on *The Merv Griffin Show*, the guest was a bodybuilder. During the interview, Merv asked, "Why do you develop those particular muscles?" The bodybuilder stepped forward and flexed a series of well-defined muscles from chest to calf. The audience applauded. "What do you use all those muscles for?" Merv asked. Again, the muscular specimen flexed, and biceps and triceps swelled to impressive proportions. "But what do you *use* those muscles for?" Merv persisted. The bodybuilder was bewildered. He didn't have an answer other than to display his well-developed frame. I was reminded that our spiritual exercises—Bible study, prayer, reading Christian books, listening to Christian radio and tapes—are also for a purpose. They're meant to strengthen our ability to build God's kingdom, not simply to improve our pose before an admiring audience.[2]

When we want to see what maturity looks like, we don't set it on a stage and let it became a sideshow of personal aggrandizement. Maturity is neatly wrapped in the priceless attribute of humility; therefore, it demonstrates itself through actions that place the attention on others—not on ourselves. If we put it on a stage, it would not flex its muscles to draw applause but would use them to benefit another. Ironically, personal development and growth is the benefit of doing for others. If all we do is for ourselves, driven by selfish ambition, we actually deplete ourselves instead of building ourselves.

What does maturity look like?

---

[2] Gary Gulbranson, *Leadership*, Summer, 1989, 43.

## *Reuben Egolf*

### 1. Maturity takes responsibility and accepts consequences without excuses.

A radio news series about honesty in America talked about excuses. The commentator said that people use three types of excuses when guilty of wrongdoing. The first is outright denial—a rejection of any involvement. Sometimes the denial comes even though the person is obviously guilty. The second is the "It's not my fault" excuse. The person looks around for someone else to blame. (Often it is a loved one—a husband or wife or parent. Sometimes it's the boss.) A third form of excuse is the "I did it, but…" approach. In this instance, the person blames circumstances for his shortcomings: he's been struggling with an illness, or the assignment wasn't clear, or the car's been giving him trouble.

Maturity does not happen without humility. Pride refuses to accept responsibility for a negative consequence because of what others may think. Humility accepts the responsibility and immediate pain of public opinion so it can learn not to repeat a mistake again. It does not sacrifice growth to preserve temporary opinion. Interestingly enough, irresponsible people tend to make the same mistakes over and over because pride is stunting the growth that correcting mistakes would produce. Maturity will never be achieved in anyone's life without correction being received.

> And the Lord God called unto Adam, and said unto him, Where art thou?
>
> And he said, I heard thy voice in the garden, and I was afraid, because I was naked; and I hid myself.
>
> And he said, Who told thee that thou wast naked? Hast thou eaten of the tree, whereof I commanded thee that thou shouldest not eat?
>
> And the man said, The woman whom thou gavest to be with me, she gave me of the tree, and I did eat.
>
> And the Lord God said unto the woman, What is this that thou hast done? And the woman said, The serpent beguiled me, and I did eat.
> **—Gen. 3:9–13 (KJV)**

It appears that not only was sin passed onto the human race, but so was the art of excuse making. In verses 14–19 we read that God holds people accountable for their actions. We could define maturity as the time when people hold themselves accountable for their actions.

Luke 15 tells the famous story of the prodigal son. His actions at the beginning of the story are the signs of immaturity. He wants his inheritance in advance and then spends without restraint, ignoring the future consequences of such action. However, on returning to his father, he displays undeniable growth when he accepts full responsibility for his actions and blames no one else for them.

We have all heard the following excuses for not going to church: there are too many hypocrites there; I don't like the songs; the sermons are too long; the seats are too hard. The list is endless. We show maturity by being able to put up with inconveniences and by being able to differentiate between a problem and inconvenience. In his book *Uh-Oh,* Robert Fulghum quotes Sigmund Wollman, a German Jew, as saying, "If you break your neck, if you have nothing to eat, if your house is on fire—then you got a problem. Everything else is inconvenience. Life *is* inconvenient. Life *is* lumpy. Learn to separate the inconveniences from the real problems. You will live longer...A lump in the oatmeal, a lump in the throat, and a lump in the breast are not the same lump. One should learn the difference."

Adolescence has a trait of classing all inconveniences as problems that need to be solved. When we see inconveniences as problems and try to solve them, we begin to overwhelm ourselves with things that really don't matter.

## 2. Maturity handles frustration, controls anger, and settles differences without violence or destruction.

> He that hath no rule over his own spirit is like a city that is broken down, and without walls.
> **—Prov. 25:28 (KJV)**

> He that is slow to anger is better than the mighty; and he that ruleth his spirit than he that taketh a city.
> **—Prov. 16:32 (KJV)**

## Reuben Egolf

The *Daily Bread* publication ran the following story in 1992.

"In the spring of 1894, the Baltimore Orioles came to Boston to play a routine baseball game. But what happened that day was anything but routine. The Orioles' John McGraw got into a fight with the Boston third baseman. Within minutes all the players from both teams had joined in the brawl. The warfare quickly spread to the grandstands. Among the fans the conflict went from bad to worse. Someone set fire to the stands and the entire ballpark burned to the ground. Not only that, but the fire spread to 107 other Boston buildings as well."[3]

Being unable to handle frustration not only affects us, but releasing frustration in the form of words spoken with a bad attitude starts a fire. Those words then become flaming darts of offense that divide and destroy relationships we hold dear.

> Even so the tongue is a little member, and boasteth great things. Behold, how great a matter a little fire kindleth!

---
3 *Daily Bread*, August 13, 1992.

> And the tongue is a fire, a world of iniquity: so is the tongue among our members, that it defileth the whole body, and setteth on fire the course of nature; and it is set on fire of hell.
>
> **—James 3:5–6**

James also said that we should be slow to speak. We must understand that we should not speak out every thought the instant it hits our mind.

Robert E. Lee said, "I cannot trust a man to control others who cannot control himself." One of the greatest requirements of being promoted to leadership and authority is having self-control. If leaders do not have self-control, they will not only destroy themselves but all others below them in the chain of authority. For example, a pastor has a God-given position and authority. He is looked up to and honored; the people have given him access to the inner sanctums of their hearts to influence them. If a person in the backseat having no position of influence self-destructs and loses control, only the individual will be affected. However, if the pastor loses self-control, not only is he affected, but so is the entire congregation. This is why the Apostle Paul saturated the three pastoral

Epistles with qualifications showing that a prospective leader possesses self-control.

## 3. Maturity patiently postpones self-gratification, passing up immediate pleasure in favor of long-term gain.

A pig ate his fill of acorns under an oak tree and then started to root around the tree. A crow remarked, "You should not do this. If you lay bare the roots, the tree will wither and die."

"Let it die," said the pig. "Who cares as long as there are acorns?"[4]

What is the difference between the mature and immature? The mature make decisions that create the future they desire. The immature make decisions that create the present they desire, while ignoring all future consequences. An immature teenager may desire the promise of a night of sexual gratification, without entertaining any thought of the long-term consequences or of the responsibility of raising a child for the next eighteen years. A mature person will weigh eighteen

---

4 *Bits & Pieces*, February, 1990, p. 24.

years against one night in the balance and make a choice that benefits God's reputation. The immature decide to get married based on a present feeling. The mature decide to get married after evaluating character for the future. Before, not after, getting married, we have to decide if marriage is something we can live with forever, or if we will we try to change it.

Moses is a case study in postponing immediate gratification for long-term gain. He could have enjoyed all that Egypt had to offer him: being the most powerful ruler in the world, living in a pristine palace, having overwhelming wealth, and leaving a lasting legacy etched on the walls of human history. However, eighty years here somehow do not compare to the endless ages of time.

> By faith Moses, when he was come to years, refused to be called the son of Pharaoh's daughter;
>
> Choosing rather to suffer affliction with the people of God, than to enjoy the pleasures of sin for a season;

Esteeming the reproach of Christ greater riches than the treasures in Egypt: for he had respect unto the recompence of the reward.

By faith he forsook Egypt, not fearing the wrath of the king: for he endured, as seeing him who is invisible.
**—Heb. 11:24–27 (KJV)**

Self-control is evidence of faith and the Holy Spirit in our lives, according to Galatians 5:22–23. The absence of self-control is catastrophic. Consider the consequences of the lack of self-control in these episodes:

- Eve and Adam eat forbidden fruit—disobey God (Gen. 3:17–19).
- Cain kills Abel—does not control his envy and jealousy (Gen. 4).
- Esau trades birthright for porridge—does not control his hunger (Gen. 25:29–34).
- Lot's wife turns into pillar of salt—does not control longings (Gen. 19:15–26).
- Abraham has child with servant-girl, Hagar, rather than waiting upon God's promise with Sarah. Ishmael and Hagar

are sent away, and wars continue to this day as a result (Gen. 16:2).
- Moses kills an Egyptian—doesn't exercise forbearance and restraint. He seeks to exact justice that was not his to render (Exod. 2:14.).
- Moses strikes the rock—doesn't control impatience (Num. 20:1–12).
- David's adultery with Bathsheba and murder of her husband—doesn't control his sexual appetites, or his desire to go to any length to give into them (2 Sam. 11:1–27, chapter 14).
- Peter's impulsive blow to soldier's ear when Jesus is arrested in the Garden of Gethsemane (Luke 22:49–51).[5]

4. **Maturity perseveres, going forward in spite of opposition and discouraging setbacks.**

Remember those earlier days after you had received the light, when you stood your ground in a great contest in the face of suffering.

---

[5] "Bible Verses about Self-Control," http://devotionalchristian.com/self-control-bible-verses.

> Sometimes you were publicly exposed to insult and persecution; at other times you stood side by side with those who were so treated.
> **—Heb. 10:32–33 (NIV)**

The size of the problem reveals the level of our maturity. If a flat tire ruins someone's life for three days, that is an indicator of where the person is in maturity.

The face of maturity never is more apparent than when it stands fearlessly in the face of persecution. It doesn't blink, and it's able to discern that opposition indicates that something great is going to be achieved.

The secret is being convinced that what we're doing is the right thing. We should never persevere in something knowing that it's not right, or that we are making a mistake. In doing so, we are being not patient and persevering but stubborn, arrogant, and obstinate.

When we set out to expand the church I pastor, Mount Calvary Tabernacle, we thought that a farmer's field near the existing church was the answer for our growth. I knew in my heart with no doubt that expanding the sanctuary of the church was the right thing to do. However, how to achieve that goal was another story. We faced setback after setback. There was an issue over ownership of the land. The property didn't pass the perc test. The state of Pennsylvania was not keen on the limited sight distance between two rolling hills that would have been near the proposed entrance. Finally, the entire deal fell through.

The church prayed and sought God, and I had a meeting some time later with a local construction company. It was determined we would build on the existing property. The project of building on the existing property went smoothly, and we ended up with a beautiful church to worship in. This process began in 2007 and was not completed until we moved in on January 15, 2010. Even though there were many inconveniences and letdowns along the way, the church as a whole maintained patience and a good attitude about persevering in the project. One's attitude during difficult situations is a key element of patience.

The Holy Spirit, not our circumstances, produces joy in our hearts.

My brethren, count it all joy when ye fall into divers temptations;

Knowing this, that the trying of your faith worketh patience.

But let patience have her perfect work, that ye may be perfect and entire, wanting nothing.
   **—James 1:2–4 (KJV)**

James 1:2 says, "My brethren, count it all joy when you fall into divers [that is, multiple or various] temptations." Those temptations can include trials, testings, hardships, tribulations, and adversities. All of these things are basically encapsulated in the word "temptations."

Counting difficulties as joy goes against the grain of the human psyche—against the human way of thinking and understanding. In the fallen condition, no sane person would ever consider it a joyful thing to fall into adversities or learn of bad news or something opposing them. The world would never consider that in the sense of joy.

It is not that Christians consider the circumstance or the situation to be a joy-producing experience.

## Please Grow Up!

That's not what God is talking about. What God is talking about is that we have joy that is literally produced by the Holy Spirit, which is evidence of his existence in our lives. It is one of the fruits of the Spirit. In other words, we as Christians do not depend on experiences to produce joy in us. We depend on the Holy Spirit to produce it in us, regardless of the circumstance. We should always look at the end or the goal of God in knowing that we need to look out into the future, and let it produce obedience in the present.

Therefore, we need to look past the present experience and look ahead at what this experience is going to produce, long-term, in our lives. Even though for the present it hurts, in the long-term, this experience can be a tool in producing maturity. As Hebrews 12 says about Jesus, "For the joy that was set before him, he did not laugh going to the cross."

What he did see was there was a resurrection coming three days later. That produced continued obedience in the present against the hurt and the pain of the nails and the spikes and the spears and the persecution of the Romans and the Jews. Therefore, what he kept in his mind was, "Yes, it is not a happy time right now, but there's joy in my heart because I can envision the future. In three days, I'm coming up out of here, and I'm defeating the devil, sin, and hell. God's people are going to have victory for the first time."

We must follow the example of Jesus. He endured the temptation of the cross because three days later, victory was coming. Even though we may be facing troubles now, we must look at the future. God will not abandon us in the middle of the problem. He has a purpose in the problem that will fulfill a greater destiny in our future. We'll be better for it once we make it to the other side.

Spiritually speaking, a valley is not where we want to live. We don't put up a tent, build a house, and raise two children in the valley. We are supposed to go *through* spiritual valleys, not live there. People who are chronic complainers actually enjoy the valley because they want something to complain about.

Sometimes people who chronically complain are not looking for us to give them an answer or a solution to their problem. They just want us to feel sorry for them as they camp out in a place where they're not supposed to live. Maturity does not tolerate a valley as a place of residence. Maturity says, "There is a mountaintop coming. We just need to keep walking."

You see, this is what James 3 is saying. When we start out knowing this, the knowledge is essential to the growth of the Christian. Ignorance gives satanic power the license to destroy us. "My people are destroyed for the lack of knowledge" (Hosea 4:6).

When God said, "You're being destroyed because of your ignorance," it was not because the people had a low IQ. It was because they turned their eyes away from the solution of God's prophetic word and said, "We're going to do it our way." We see people today in the church living this way too often. We'll do it our way and never break open the Bread of Life. We become ignorant and give license to the devil to wreak havoc in our lives. Then we complain that we're in the situation we're in, but it's because of our neglecting to eat the Bread of Life.

This is knowledge for the heart and for the mind and the soul to find its navigation compass in this spiritual life. So if we didn't know this, we would complain and find fault with God. But James 3 tells us, because we *do* know this, because we know God is going to do something greater in our lives as a result of it, we're not going to complain about it. If we do, we're saying, "God, you don't know what you're doing."

James 3 says, "Knowing this, that the trying of your faith…" If we're knowing this, that our faith is being tested, is being put to the fire, then what happens? That knowledge "worketh patience," or develops it. It works it. Praise God for working it!

Aren't we glad when we can work our bodies? What do we do when we work our bodies? We develop muscle. When God works our faith, we develop spiritual muscle.

"Knowing this, that the trying of your faith worketh patience." We all know what patience is. Patience isn't merely tolerating something. Patience is a joyful perseverance. In other words, it's not just putting up with it, grumbling all the way. That's not patience. Patience has a joyous attitude and demeanor, even while it's going through hardship. It may not be laughing like a hyena, but it isn't growling, either.

Now look at verse 4. "But let…" Allow. That's our part. We have to permit this to happen. "But let patience have her perfect work that ye may be perfect and entire, wanting nothing." Patience wants to work perfectly and completely in our lives.

In other words, we can come to the mature place of literally not being deficient. That's a lofty goal for the Christian. We can reach that place in this lifetime. That doesn't mean we'll never make a mistake or a misstep.

According to the Bible, in the maturing process, we *can* become complete and entire beings. We can actually become fully efficient and equipped and be mature, responsible children of God so he can count on us in any adverse situation when he wants to demonstrate his power through our lives.

### 5. Maturity faces offenses and disappointment without becoming bitter.

Adversity should act as a hammer with a nail. The harder I'm hit, the deeper I should go.

Ultimately, it's my choice how I react to a problem. The Apostle Paul, in 2 Corinthians 11–12, reveals the choice he made to develop maturity and depend upon the Lord even more. Let's look at what he went through first, according to 1 Corinthians 11:23–27: He worked hard in the face of opposition to start churches and was repeatedly beaten and imprisoned for his faith. In Philippi, he spent two years in a cell containing his own feces. People he trusted betrayed him. He was without food and water on many occasions. He had many near-death experiences: he was stoned and left for dead, and he was left in the water for a night and day when his ship was destroyed.

How many of us would have gone through the same things without complaining? Someone talks about us or doesn't shake our hand, and we are ready to quit the church and pity ourselves into oblivion. Life without persecution, hardships, suffering, and all forms of adversity is a fairy tale. The reality is that life is tough. Either we learn to deal with it, or it will grind us to powder. Either we grow up, or we resort to the misery of perpetual immaturity maintained by excuses and complaining.

When we look at biblical characters, we often think of them as supermen and superwomen who were in another class of human beings. The truth of the matter is that these individuals stood out as a result of their faith in God and decision making. Having been shaped by their decisions, their lives were extraordinary. We can have the same life as they had if we make the same decisions they did.

Let's see what Paul did in response to these chaotic events in his life.

> And lest I should be exalted above measure through the abundance of the revelations, there was given to me a thorn in the flesh, the messenger of Satan to buffet me, lest I should be exalted above measure.
>
> For this thing I besought the Lord thrice, that it might depart from me.
>
> And he said unto me, My grace is sufficient for thee: for my strength is made perfect in weakness. Most gladly therefore will I rather glory in my infirmities, that the power of Christ may rest upon me.
>
> Therefore I take pleasure in infirmities, in reproaches, in necessities, in persecutions,

in distresses for Christ's sake: for when I am weak, then am I strong.
**—2 Cor. 12:7–10 (KJV)**

The "thorn in the flesh" that many people have tried to explain as a sickness, an eye disease, or some other physical ailment is clearly stated to be an angel of Satan. This unnamed being has been sent to harass Paul in the form of the experiences listed in 1 Corinthians 11:23–28. The great apostle could have let these experiences drive him into despair and depression, and away from God. However, he just turned the steering wheel and permitted the experiences to drive him deeper in his dependency on God. It was that simple— a decision! Immaturity reveals itself by making wrong decisions and then complaining that it lives a subpar life. Complaining is one of the most fruitless exercises we can ever indulge in. It does nothing to change the situation; it's a waste of time; it feeds and nourishes irresponsibility; it ultimately infects our own soul with bitterness. However, one of the worst attributes of complaining is that when we complain, we're actually saying, "God, you don't know what you're doing," or "I don't trust you!" Then, we create a future that is all about us and not about Christ living through us.

## 6. Maturity shows humility.

A mature person can say, "I was wrong." He is also able to say, "I am sorry." And when he is proven right, he does not have to say, "I told you so." Humility loses the right of self-vindication and vengeance. It will not evidence itself by being satisfied with another's deserved pain. Humility quickly forgives without payment and looks forward to the future and puts the past where it belongs—in the past.

> I write unto you, fathers, because ye have known him that is from the beginning. I write unto you, young men, because ye have overcome the wicked one. I write unto you, little children, because ye have known the Father.
>
> I have written unto you, fathers, because ye have known him that is from the beginning. I have written unto you, young men, because ye are strong, and the word of God abideth in you, and ye have overcome the wicked one.
> **—1 John 2:13–14 (KJV)**

When I was a child, I spake as a child, I understood as a child, I thought as a child: but when I became a man, I put away childish things.
**—1 Cor. 13:11 (KJV)**

The above Scriptures reveal characteristics associated with each phase of life. As David Breese says, "Strong sons of God are not perfected by childish pursuits."

Maturity values principles and character more than emotions and opinions.

In the political arena today, we have a tendency to base decisions on emotions instead of the rule of law. Our politicians seem to sacrifice the law to gain supposed popularity. They are forgetting that the law is a set of standards to be upheld to ensure success. Many are parading the stories of parents or spouses residing in the United States illegally and whom are about to be deported. These relatives want to remain with their family members who are legal citizens. Their sad stories play on the human heart, and the politicians exclaim, "This is inhumane, and these families deserve to remain intact!" Then when a person stands up and states the fact that there are standards to be met before legal entry, that person is labeled as a hater of people of another national origin. No, that is a person who isn't afraid to tell the truth! We have standards set by the rule of law. People must not be afraid to stand up and tell the truth, regardless of how they may be perceived. When a politician sells his soul for popularity and the truth to the highest bidder, that, my friends, is a dangerous man! The judges on *American Idol* will tell a performer, "That was not good enough to make it on the show." The singer sulks back home, and the family exclaims, "That's not right; you have a beautiful voice, you're a nice person, and Mr. Cowell is just mean!" No, he is not mean; the fact is that the show has standards, and they must be met.

Let's shift gears to the spiritual. The same phenomenon has entered the church. Leaders are sacrificing standards for increased popularity and membership. Some pastors now say, "This member is a nice person who loves the Lord." However, his or her lifestyle is contrary to the standard of living prescribed by the Bible. Pastors are afraid to stand up for the truth; therefore, a lot of illegals are infiltrating the church. Now their culture is being implemented in the house of God, and it is changing the standard of God's kingdom. The standard of God is to produce and maintain the culture within the church. Our nation is being changed by not upholding its laws, and the same change is happening in the church. The pastors of America have to go back and fall in love with the truth again instead of with themselves! If a pastor tells people they are wrong, it doesn't mean that he hates them, but that he has chosen to uphold the standard of God over their feelings and opinions. People simply need to meet the standard of God, and as a result, they will enjoy the benefits that meeting his standard will produce in them. Truth is not relative. Truth is based on the word of God, not on emotion or feelings. Sometimes the truth hurts because it has found rebellion in the heart. If truth were based on our feelings, then there would be no anchor to hold onto because they would be shifting continuously. Thank God for the truth that never changes!

When people say they want revival, they mean they want their preacher to give them many nights of hair-raising manifestations attributed to the Holy Spirit that will entertain them and make them think they are holy enough that God would do this before them. What they forget is the majority of the most memorable manifestations of the Holy Spirit throughout history have been before sinners, but they never seem to make the connection. Instead they walk out with a jerk or shake that proves they are spiritual, but their mostly nonexistent prayer life, Bible reading, and time spent with God remains unchanged. Spiritual maturity does not chase goose bumps but instead cherishes the rewards of obedience in the inner man. Even if there is no supposed outward manifestation of someone being slain in the spirit, or one physically vibrating, the mature person will leave the church service satisfied because of hearing the word of God presented as a challenge for a deeper experience with the Lord Jesus Christ.

Today we think of love and marriage as an emotional experience, as opposed to a commitment, and when we aren't having those lovey-dovey feelings anymore, we think our marriage is broken. People who live in a system where arranged marriages are common have a different outlook. This is not to say they don't experience love, emotional feelings, or excitement about their marriages, but those feelings are not primary. They are secondary to the commitment or arrangement. We see this same phenomenon in the church. When initial fuzzy feelings subside, then people may think the relationship with Christ is broken and stop attending church. They fail to understand that feelings are secondary to the commitment to Jesus Christ. I have seen people pray to get back the feeling they had when they were first saved. They return to the altar for the same thing over and over because, when that feeling subsides, they believe the relationship is leaving with it. So they are good for a couple of months, and then they have to pray to regain the "high" feeling. This process is repeated over and over. When we grow up, we realize it's not about feelings per se but the decision we have made to stick with a commitment. What will get us through a tough time is not the feelings we experience but rather the commitment we have made. If we want to pray for a feeling, we should pray until we get the same conviction and resolve we had when we were persuaded that Christ was the only answer to our dilemma of sin. Feelings and moods change, but our commitment should be that which keeps us on an even keel.

Immature leadership has the common trait of indecisiveness. Decisiveness is the number-one quality of a leader. Decisive people do not fill their sails with the wind of popular opinion but rather are driven by personal conviction and resolve. When a leader is clear about their values and goals, it will be much easier for him or her to make decisions firmly. Paul said in 1 Timothy that church leadership should consist of new converts and that they should be first proven before entering an office of authority. The maturing process must take place to remove the immature weaknesses and pitfalls due to pride from being the ambition of the soul. When leaders aspire for a title and live for attention, when they go home at night satisfied after hearing applause, when they become intoxicated with who they are, then we will no longer hear our leadership making decisions out of resolve, conviction, values, and honoring principles. They will become nothing more than programmed responses echoing popular opinion. However, that's not leadership!

The world is in desperate need of parents who value principle over the whims of their children! Children need parents to act like adults. There is nothing more repulsive than seeing a forty-something mother wearing her teenage daughter's clothing. Children don't need their mom or dad to be a friend—they need them to be a parent! Mature parents should be concerned with the success of the child more than with the affection of the child. Parenting is not being an ol' buddy but a foreman of construction. When we decide to have a child, we must take the responsibility to form that child. A friend loves us the way we are...but a father and mother love us too much to leave us the way we are. A friend will ignore our weaknesses... A parent will deal with them and remove them. Sometimes this process hurts, but the momentary pain is miniscule compared to the long-term effect.

## CHAPTER FOUR

# The Agents God Uses for Growth

Growth and maturity do not occur naturally. The babe in Christ requires sound and consistent "spiritual pediatrics," and God uses certain agents to bring about spiritual growth to bring us to deeper and deeper maturity in Christ. The word is obviously a key and necessary element for spiritual growth (1 Pet. 1:23–2:3; 2 Pet. 1:3–4; 3:18; John 17:17). In John 17:17, the Lord prayed for the church and said, "Sanctify them through your word, your word is truth." The reference to "sanctify" or sanctification is fundamentally a synonym for growth and maturity and expresses the Lord's objective for all believers. Other agents that God uses to bring about spiritual growth include:

1. Church leaders (Eph. 4:11ff.; 1 Thess. 5:12; James 5:14)
2. The care and concern of the body of Christ as a whole (Eph. 4:16; 1 Thess. 5:11ff.)
3. Suffering or the trials of life (James 1:2–5; 1 Pet. 1:6; Ps. 119:67, 71, 75, 92)
4. Last, but not least, the indwelling and teaching ministry of the Holy Spirit (Eph. 3:16ff.; 1 Cor. 2:6–3:4)[6]

The following is taken from *The Complete Book of Everyday Christianity: An A-To-Z Guide To Following Christ in Every Aspect of Life*. It gives one of the best descriptions for growth and its requirements using biblical metaphors.

## Metaphors of Growth

In the Bible there are four major metaphors of spiritual growth.

*The seed—an agricultural metaphor.* Growth includes germination, development, transitions, fruition, and multiplication. In his public teaching, Jesus used the seed metaphor for the life of

---

[6] "Marks of Maturity: Biblical Characteristics of a Christian Leader," https://bible.org/series/marks-maturity-biblical-characteristics-christian-leader.

the kingdom sown into the soil of people's hearts (Matt. 13:4) and for the sowing of the children of the kingdom into the world (Matt. 13:38).

*The child—a biological metaphor.* Paul used this term for the Corinthians (1 Cor. 3:1) because of their schismatic behavior and their infantile dependence on human teachers. In fact, he says, they are still "on the bottle" needing milk (1 Cor. 3:2). The author of Hebrews uses the same metaphor for another community stalled in a no-growth life (Heb. 5:12–13). Tragically many Christians run off to this and that conference being blown about by every wind of doctrine (Eph. 4:14) and never learn to feed themselves or others. Just as infants learn to feed themselves, just as children move from total dependency to interdependency, just as young people move from a hand-me-down and secondhand faith to an adult faith of their own, so we grow spiritually.

*The disciple—an educational metaphor.* In the ancient world disciples were learners who formed a deepening relationship with their master. The purpose was not merely the transmission of information. When the disciple is fully trained, Jesus said, the disciple "will be like the teacher" (Luke

6:40 NRSV)—an imitation process. So discipleship involves development from mere service to friendship with God—a transition that is parallel to one Paul explored frequently: from slavery to sonship and being an heir. In one sense we never move beyond obedience, but the obedience changes character from simply "doing what we are told" to doing God's will because we have increasingly the mind of Christ. This is the heart of *guidance.*

*The building—an architectural metaphor.* "You are God's field, God's building" (1 Cor. 3:9). Once again he is thinking of the people of God and not merely a collection of individual saints. God's people are really the temple of God—a living building that grows increasingly into a sanctuary in which God's Spirit lives (1 Cor. 3:16). Christ is the foundation of that building (1 Cor. 3:11), and though Christ is the ultimate living stone, each of us is adding to the structure stone upon stone. Peter says we are being built "into a spiritual house" (1 Pet. 2:5). We are like a medieval cathedral that is always being built and never quite finished. Who is doing the building? Who makes the house grow?

*Reuben Egolf*

## Cultivating Growth

The seed develops. The infant matures. The disciple learns. The building is being built. But all four metaphors show that growth requires human cooperation. In fact *both* God and the stones make the temple grow, but it is mainly God's continuing work of transformation. From first to last, from conception to resurrection, from germination to harvest, from laying the foundation to the completion of the temple, spiritual growth is primarily the achievement of God: we are God's workmanship.

Growth, however, is not automatic. God seeks our cooperation. We are fellow workers with God (1 Cor. 3:9). Paul thanks God that the faith and love of the Thessalonians are "growing more and more" (2 Thess. 1:3). He warns Timothy that some have given up the good fight and "have shipwrecked their faith" (1 Tim. 1:19). The author of Hebrews repeatedly warns his readers to be careful not to drift away from the faith (Heb. 2:1) and not to fall short of true sabbath rest in Christ (Heb. 4:1). We must persevere in growth (Heb. 10:36). It is literally grow or die![7]

---

[7] Robert Banks & R. Paul Stevens, eds., *The Complete Book of Everyday Christianity: An A-To-Z Guide To Following Christ in Every Aspect of Life* (Chicago; Graceworks, 2011).

## Please Grow Up!

And he gave some, apostles; and some, prophets; and some, evangelists; and some, pastors and teachers;

For the perfecting of the saints, for the work of the ministry, for the edifying of the body of Christ:

Till we all come in the unity of the faith, and of the knowledge of the Son of God, unto a perfect man, unto the measure of the stature of the fulness of Christ:

That we henceforth be no more children, tossed to and fro, and carried about with every wind of doctrine, by the sleight of men, and cunning craftiness, whereby they lie in wait to deceive;

But speaking the truth in love, may grow up into him in all things, which is the head, even Christ:
**—Eph. 4:11–15 (KJV)**

Tumbleweed is a plant that breaks away from its roots and is driven about by the wind as a light rolling mass, scattering seeds as it goes. Tumbleweed believers have not allowed their roots to sink deep into the truth. When some people encounter a trial or hardship, they snap off from the word, and away they go, blown by the wind of adversity. Not only do they go summersaulting across the landscape of life, but they also begin to deposit seeds of fruitlessness in others. Spreading the reasons for their faithlessness, they attribute it to others and never take personal responsibility. Tumbleweed believers run from church to church if confronted over their sin. I have witnessed too many leaving the church, not because of moral failure in leadership or some other atrocity, but simply because they were confronted over sin. How will we grow if we are not able to receive correction to remove whatever is hindering our growth?

Another observation is that tumbleweed is quick to catch fire but just as quick to burn out! We have all seen this phenomenon. A person blows into church and catches fire and appears to be the next pillar of the house, only to quickly fade and disappear.

Maturity really comes down to this: a commitment to see things through to completion. In spite of the obstacles that hinder us, problems that assail our progress, and distractions that discourage us, we remain focused on the goal set before us. Maturity is a loftier goal than the accumulation of money, prestigious employment, and people's favorable opinions of us. In the end, maturity is the quality of soul that we can't have integrity without. Donald Creighton said, "History is the record of an encounter between character and circumstance." What will be our historical record?

# About the Author

Reuben Egolf has been the pastor of Mount Calvary Tabernacle in Williamson, Pennsylvania, for eighteen years. He was president and cofounder of Mount Calvary International Ministerial Fellowship (MCIMF) from 2003–2010.

God has given Reuben the privilege of being the host of *Experience Life Today* (www.explife.org), a television program he and his wife, Laci, launched together in 2009. This program confronts everyday issues with the word of God. It currently airs in four states.

Reuben has authored three books: *Can You Trust God,* dealing with the sovereignty of God; *The Voice Within,* dealing with the conscience; and *Avoiding Relationship Mayhem,* exposing the pitfalls of relationships that need to be avoided.

## Please Grow Up!

Recently, Reuben was installed as the new Washington, DC, capital director for the US National Prayer Council, an organization dedicated to mobilizing pastors and prayer leaders to lead the church back to prayer concerning the pertinent issues of our time. Learn more about the US National Prayer Council at www.usnationalprayercouncil.com.

Made in the USA
Middletown, DE
22 March 2015